MAY 2017

SandCastle

Rhyme Time

A Career for Mr. Lear

Anders Hanson

Consulting Editor, Diane Craig, M.A./Reading Specialist

ABDO
Publishing Company

Published by ABDO Publishing Company, 4940 Viking Drive, Edina, Minnesota 55435.

Printed in the United States.

Credits
Edited by: Pam Price
Curriculum Coordinator: Nancy Tuminelly
Cover and Interior Design and Production: Mighty Media
Photo Credits: BananaStock Ltd., Comstock, Corel, Digital Vision, Hemera, PhotoDisc, Stockbyte

Library of Congress Cataloging-in-Publication Data

Hanson, Anders, 1980-
     A career for Mr. Lear / Anders Hanson.
        p. cm. -- (Rhyme time)
     Includes index.
     ISBN 1-59197-779-7 (hardcover)
     ISBN 1-59197-885-8 (paperback)
     1. English language--Rhyme--Juvenile literature. I. Title: Career for Mister Lear. II. Title.
III. Rhyme time (ABDO Publishing Company)

PE1517.H34 2004
428.1'3--dc22
                                                                                    2004049514

SandCastle™ books are created by a professional team of educators, reading specialists, and content developers around five essential components that include phonemic awareness, phonics, vocabulary, text comprehension, and fluency. All books are written, reviewed, and leveled for guided reading, early intervention reading, and Accelerated Reader® programs and designed for use in shared, guided, and independent reading and writing activities to support a balanced approach to literacy instruction.

Let Us Know

After reading the book, SandCastle would like you to tell us your stories about reading. What is your favorite page? Was there something hard that you needed help with? Share the ups and downs of learning to read. We want to hear from you! To get posted on the ABDO Publishing Company Web site, send us e-mail at:

sandcastle@abdopub.com

SandCastle Level: Fluent

Words that rhyme do not have to be spelled the same. These words rhyme with each other:

appear

near

career

pier

cashier

souvenir

fear

steer

gear

tear

After school the students
wait outside for the school bus
to appear.

Mikey, Drew, and Joseph are each dressed for a different career.

If a movie has a scary scene,
Vicki knows that it's just a movie
and there is nothing to **fear**.

Anthony and Meggie's mom pays the **cashier**.

Elijah and his dad pack up their camping gear.

William and his dad get ready to fish off the pier.

Linda likes to play at the park **near** her house.

Sammy went to the beach
and found a starfish to keep as
a **souvenir**.

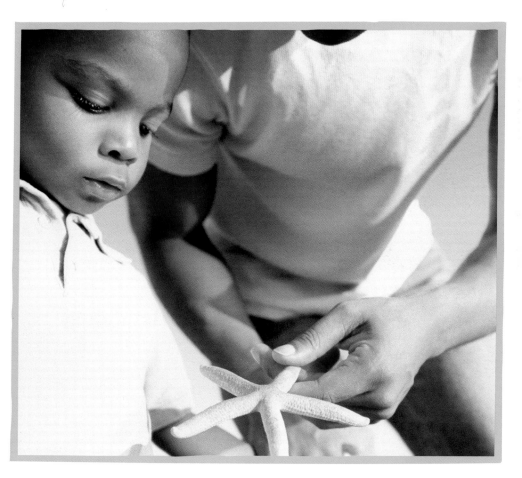

Chuck is sad.

A tear rolls down his cheek.

Alexandra is learning how to ride her bike.

Her mom helps her **steer**.

A Career
for Mr. Lear

Mr. Lear is in search of a career.
He wanted to be a puppeteer,
but the audience never did appear.

He thought about being an auctioneer, but his voice was not loud enough for people to hear.

He wanted to be a cashier,
but he was not happy selling gear.

Mr. Lear tried raising steer,
but he could not keep them near.

Mr. Lear shed a tear.
Then he said, "Never fear!
I will soon find
the right career!"

Finally, Mr. Lear
became an engineer.

Now it was clear
he had found the right career.

After a year, Mr. Lear
was the world's premier engineer.

He was filled with cheer!

Rhyming Riddle

What do you call
a keepsake bought on a dock?

Pier souvenir

Glossary

auctioneer. someone who sells items at an auction

engineer. someone who is trained to design and build structures such as machines, cars, or roads

pier. a platform that extends over a body of water

puppeteer. someone who operates puppets to entertain others

souvenir. something you keep to remind you of a person, place, or event

steer. a young, male cow raised for beef; to control the direction a vehicle travels in

About SandCastle™

A professional team of educators, reading specialists, and content developers created the SandCastle™ series to support young readers as they develop reading skills and strategies and increase their general knowledge. The SandCastle™ series has four levels that correspond to early literacy development in young children. The levels are provided to help teachers and parents select the appropriate books for young readers.

Emerging Readers
(no flags)

Beginning Readers
(1 flag)

Transitional Readers
(2 flags)

Fluent Readers
(3 flags)

These levels are meant only as a guide. All levels are subject to change.

To see a complete list of SandCastle™ books and other nonfiction titles from ABDO Publishing Company, visit www.abdopub.com or contact us at:
4940 Viking Drive, Edina, Minnesota 55435 • 1-800-800-1312 • fax: 1-952-831-1632